Coventry Kersey Dighton Patmore, Alice Christiana Thompson
Meynell

The Poetry of Pathos and Delight

From the works of Coventry Patmore

Coventry Kersey Dighton Patmore, Alice Christiana Thompson Meynell

The Poetry of Pathos and Delight
From the works of Coventry Patmore

ISBN/EAN: 9783337251567

Printed in Europe, USA, Canada, Australia, Japan

Cover: Foto ©Thomas Meinert / pixelio.de

More available books at **www.hansebooks.com**

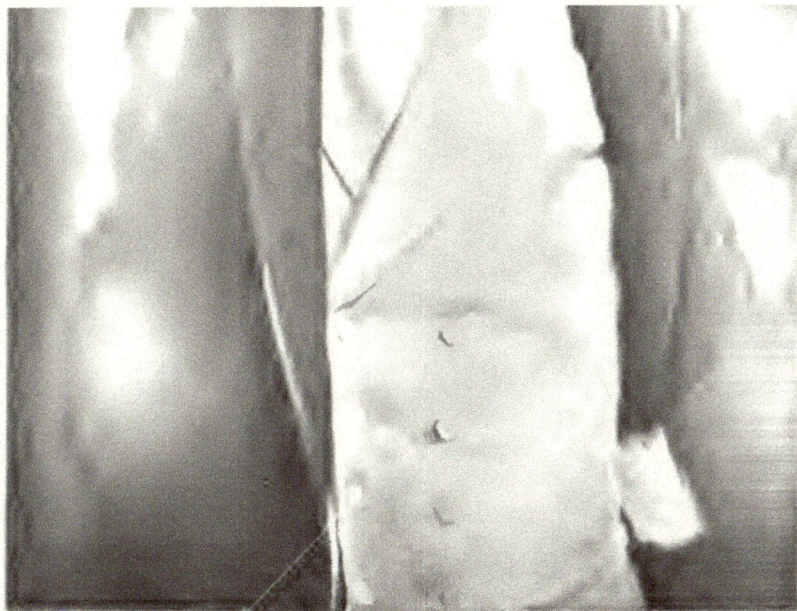

Coventry Patmore

THE POETRY OF
PATHOS & DELIGHT

From the Works of

COVENTRY PATMORE

Passages Selected by

ALICE MEYNELL

WITH A PORTRAIT AFTER J. S. SARGENT, A.R.A.

LONDON: WILLIAM HEINEMANN
MDCCCXCVI

INTRODUCTORY NOTE

THIS book does not offer a selection in the usual sense. The poetry of a master is selected before it is written, and before it is conceived; and the mind that conceives it is selected. Mr. Coventry Patmore's art and labour do but second that original distinction. Therefore it is hardly necessary to say that my intention has not been to make a collection of "best passages." What has been intended is to collect passages in which the poet has dealt with two things—delight and sorrow, those human and intelligible passions to which all real poetry has access, but which this poetry touches so close as to be mingled with them and changed into them.

So to offer great poetry to the natural human sensibility, should be to gain for the poet's whole work new readers. I confess that is my motive.

INTRODUCTORY NOTE

Because of their youth, which has not allowed them to read very much, or because of accident, there may be many readers still to gain. Among them may be the fittest—not the less fit because they have been for a time under the influence of a fashion for inordinate haste, or for inordinate leisure, of appreciation. Mr. Patmore's greatest work is neither so new as to gratify the eagerness of one fashion, nor so old as to flatter the reluctance of the other. It is a work of the beginning of the last quarter of our century. It is dated later than Mr. Swinburne's best, for instance, but it had its place in literature before the present young love of poetry had taken life. Again, many poets are heard because a chorus of contemporaries sings with them and like them. Mr. Coventry Patmore's voice is single in his day, and single in our literature. It makes part of no choir loud by numbers, and so it needs an attentive ear. To that attentive ear it sounds alone, as the divinest voice of our time.

There is a dignity in Mr. Patmore's reputation (attendant on the exceeding dignity of his art) that might be offended—though it could not be injured—by officious praises. But it is not inopportune to say thus much : Readers of this book and of the entire poems may be promised a perfect respite from the tedious controversy as to matter and manner, thought and expression. They shall not be invited to attend to discussions as to the relative importance of two things that in truth have no high importance if they can be divided so as to be merely related. The dispute is an inconsiderable one ; it is perfectly opportune in the criticism of all poetry below a certain perfectly definite standard of art, and there only. Above that standard, thought and form are not opposed, nor merely related ; they are one. It is not difficult to make a definition of classical poetry, if classical poetry may rightly be defined as all poetry—be its thought what it may, and its form what it may—in which thought and form are one. Classical poetry of every age—and every age has had a little—is that in which there is no antithesis, in which there is more than a bond—union and fusion. The classical poem may be a mere " To Althea from Prison," or even a mere " To Blossoms." In the small classic the word is fused with its fancy, and in the great it is fused with its passion ; and the greater the passion the greater the splendour of the fire of that fusion—the " integrity of fire."

The more essential passages of Mr. Coventry Patmore's much earlier work—*The Angel in the House*—are classic, and very high in that noble rank. He plays with this power of his art in the brief metre, the symmetrical stanza, and the colloquial phrase. He has here accepted the dailiest things and made them spirit and fire. There has been something said against these colloquialisms ; and indeed they would not be tolerable in hands less austere and sweet. The newest Philistine, who is afraid of the reproach of Philistinism, who denies Philistinism in the name of a Philistine, and ultimately receives a Philistine's reward, has been known to make light of some of Mr. Patmore's couplets, which he finds too "domestic." But such "domestic" couplets as those in "Olympus," for instance, are a smiling defiance of Philistinism. So are the brilliant stanzas, made of life, sense, and spirit, in which the very accessories,—the spoilt accessories—of a modern English wedding are rendered grave and blithe, and the bridegroom is restored to the dignity of the sun. Mr. Patmore makes the Wedding Sermon (at the close of *The Angel in the House*) the improbable opportunity for the finest wit and thought, tenderness, mystery, and celestial knowledge. One of the things that have baffled the trivial in these early poems is probably what they have taken for triviality or artlessness in the metre as well as in the word. Locks and bars and bolts are less secure for the locking away of a poet's privacy, than is his unintelligible candour. In his solemnity the world recognises a mystery; but by his frank play and simplicity it is sometimes baffled and misled into disregard.

The *Odes* are greater than the earlier poems, because they have greater capacity for the quality that is in all Mr. Patmore's work. As for their metre, it is their very poetry. They move with indescribable dignity, and with the freedom of the spirit. The wind bloweth where it listeth. With absolute art the poet sighs, or pauses, or recovers breath, in the " irregular " line, with an effect of infinite liberty and pathos. " Thou hearest the sound thereof." One of Mr. Patmore's worthiest

contemporaries has said that the Odes are almost
too mournful to be read, because they are so close
to the thought: "the verse attending on the
thought, and having no independent life of its
own." This appreciation is insufficient, for there
is union rather than "attendance;" but it ex-
presses hastily the effect of this most sensitive and
vital line—precisely the effect, which, in another
art, results from the phrases of a *Parsifal*. Take
the regular stanza as answering to a symmetrical melody; you will perceive that neither
stanza nor tune can be so immediately sensitive as
are those sentences of music, and those lines of the
ode in the hands of a master. No other metrical
form could be so free and so living a communi-
cation.

What is here to be communicated is vital and
mortal pathos and felicity. Even as far as the
reader has capacity to perceive that passion, he is
aware that it is greater than his experience, and
he confesses that it was uttered out of a greater
capacity than his. Compassion with that greater
passion is a high and worthy manner of admiration.
It may be the "terror" that Aristotle joined to

" pity." Compassion in the highest degree is the divinest form of religion. The compassion of the slighter acquaintance with sorrow for the greater, and of the smaller capacity for the vaster, is a remorse of tenderness, lowliness, and respect, the paradox of worship.

Dexterity—the lower technique—may become habitual, and the more brilliant kinds of habit are often mistaken for the actual intention of great art; but great art is never habitual. Art has a perpetually living intention. All the lines and passages here gathered together are proofs of this instancy of art. And they are chosen as instant communications of the two passions of happiness and pain, because these are the most simple. It would have been easy to represent Mr. Patmore by an anthology proving him the poet of wit, or the poet of beauty, or the poet of indignation. But the most classic subject of classic poetry is the most intelligible in kind, however enormous in degree—felicity and infelicity. Of melancholy— the black humour—none of Mr. Patmore's work has a sign.

CONTENTS

xiii

CONTENTS

CONTENTS

TO THE UN-KNOWN EROS.

WHAT rumour'd heavens are these
Which not a poet sings,
O, Unknown Eros? What this breeze
Of sudden wings
Speeding at far returns of time from interstellar
    space
To fan my very face,
And gone as fleet,
Through delicatest ether feathering soft their soli-
    tary beat,
With ne'er a light plume dropp'd, nor any trace
To speak of whence they came, or whither they
    depart?
And why this palpitating heart,
This blind and unrelated joy,
This meaningless desire,
That moves me like the Child
Who in the flushing darkness troubled lies,
Inventing lonely prophecies,

TO THE UNKNOWN EROS

Which even to his Mother mild
He dares not tell;
To which himself is infidel;
His heart not less on fire
With dreams impossible as wildest Arab Tale,
(So thinks the boy,)
With dreams that turn him red and pale,
Yet less impossible and wild
Than those which bashful Love, in his own way
     and hour,
Shall duly bring to flower?
O, Unknown Eros, sire of awful bliss,
What portent and what Delphic word,
Such as in form of snake forebodes the bird,
Is this?
In me life's even flood
What eddies thus?
What in its ruddy orbit lifts the blood,
Like a perturbed moon of Uranus,
Reaching to some great world in ungauged dark-
     ness hid;
And whence
This rapture of the sense
Which, by thy whisper bid,
Reveres with obscure rite and sacramental sign
A bond I know not of nor dimly can divine:

This subject loyalty which longs
For chains and thongs
Woven of gossamer and adamant,
To bind me to my unguess'd want,
And so to lie,
Between those quivering plumes that thro' fine
     ether pant,
For hopeless, sweet eternity?
What God unhonour'd hitherto in songs,
Or which, that now
Forgettest the disguise
That Gods must wear who visit human eyes,
Art Thou?
Thou art not Amor; or, if so, yon pyre,
That waits the willing victim, flames with vestal
     fire;
Nor mooned Queen of maids; or, if thou'rt she,
Ah, then, from Thee
Let Bride and Bridegroom learn what kisses be!
In what veil'd hymn
Or mystic dance
Would he that were thy Priest advance
Thine earthly praise, thy glory limn?
Say, should the feet that feel thy thought
In double-center'd circuit run,
In that compulsive focus, Nought,

TO THE UNKNOWN EROS

In this a furnace like the sun ;
And might some note of thy renown
And high behest
Thus in enigma be expressed :
' There lies the crown
Which all thy longing cures.
Refuse it, Mortal, that it may be yours !
It is a Spirit, though it seems red gold ;
And such may no man, but by shunning, hold.
Refuse it, till refusing be despair ;
And thou shalt feel the phantom in thy hair.'

ENGLAND

Lo, weary of the greatness of her ways,
There lies my Land, with hasty pulse and
   hard,
Her ancient beauty marr'd,
And, in her cold and aimless roving sight,
Horror of light;
Sole vigour left in her last lethargy,
Save when, at bidding of some dreadful breath,
The rising death
Rolls up with force;
And then the furiously gibbering corse
Shakes, panglessly convuls'd, and sightless stares,
Whilst one Physician pours in rousing wines,
One anodynes,
And one declares
That nothing ails it but the pains of growth.
   My last look loth
Is taken; and I turn, with the relief
Of knowing that my life-long hope and grief

ENGLAND

Are surely vain,
To that unshapen time to come, when She,
A dim, heroic Nation long since dead,
The foulness of her agony forgot,
Shall all benignly shed
Through ages vast
The ghostly grace of her transfigured past
Over the present, harass'd and forlorn,
Of nations yet unborn ;
And this shall be the lot
Of those who, in the bird-voice and the
    blast
Of her omniloquent tongue,
Have truly sung
Or greatly said,
To shew as one
With those who have best done,
And be as rays,
Thro' the still altering world, around her
    changeless head.
  Therefore no 'plaint be mine
Of listeners none,
No hope of render'd use or proud reward,
In hasty times and hard ;
But chants as of a lonely thrush's throat.
At latest eve,

That does in each calm note
Both joy and grieve;
Notes few and strong and fine,
Gilt with sweet day's decline,
And sad with promise of a different sun.

REMNANT
OF HONOUR

REMNANT of Honour, brooding in the dark
Over your bitter cark,
Staring, as Rispah stared, astonied seven days
Upon the corpses of so many sons,
Who loved her once,
Dead in the dim and lion-haunted ways,
Who could have dreamt
That times should come like these !

VICTORY
IN DEFEAT

Ah, God, alas,
How soon it came to pass
The sweetness melted from thy barbed hook
Which I so simply took;
And I lay bleeding on the bitter land,
Afraid to stir against thy least command,
But losing all my pleasant life-blood, whence
Force should have been heart's frailty to withstand.
Life is not life at all without delight,
Nor has it any might;
And better than the insentient heart and brain
Is sharpest pain;
And better for the moment seems it to rebel,
If the great Master, from his lifted seat,
Ne'er whispers to the wearied servant 'Well!'
Yet what returns of love did I endure,
When to be pardon'd seem'd almost more sweet
Than aye to have been pure!
But day still faded to disastrous night,

VICTORY IN DEFEAT

And thicker darkness changed to feebler light,
Until forgiveness, without stint renew'd,
Was now no more with loving tears imbued,
Vowing no more offence.
Not less to thine Unfaithful didst thou cry,
' Come back, poor Child ; be all as 'twas before.'
But I,
' No, no ; I will not promise any more !
Yet, when I feel my hour is come to die,
And so I am secured of continence,
Then may I say, though haply then in vain,
" My only, only Love, O, take me back again !" '
 Thereafter didst thou smite
So hard that, for a space,
Uplifted seem'd Heav'n's everlasting door,
And I indeed the darling of thy grace.
But, in some dozen changes of the moon,
A bitter mockery seem'd thy bitter boon.
The broken pinion was no longer sore.
Again, indeed, I woke
Under so dread a stroke
That all the strength it left within my heart
Was just to ache and turn, and then to turn and
 ache,
And some weak sign of war unceasingly to make.
And here I lie,

With no one near to mark,
Thrusting Hell's phantoms feebly in the dark,
And still at point more utterly to die.
O God, how long !
Put forth indeed thy powerful right hand,
While time is yet,
Or never shall I see the blissful land !
    Thus I: then God, in pleasant speech and strong
(Which soon I shall forget) :
'The man who, though his fights be all defeats,
Still fights,
Enters at last
The heavenly Jerusalem's rejoicing streets
With glory more, and more triumphant rites
Than always-conquering Joshua's, when his blast
The frighted walls of Jericho down cast ;
And, lo, the glad surprise
Of peace beyond surmise,
More than in common Saints, for ever in his eyes.'

SAINT VALEN-
TINE'S DAY

WELL dost thou, Love, thy solemn Feast to hold
In vestal February;
Not rather choosing out some rosy day
From the rich coronet of the coming May,
When all things meet to marry !
   O, quick, prævernal Power
That signall'st punctual through the sleepy mould
The Snowdrop's time to flower,
Fair as the rash oath of virginity
Which is first-love's first cry ;
O, Baby Spring,
That flutter'st sudden 'neath the breast of Earth
A month before the birth ;
Whence is the peaceful poignancy,
The joy contrite,
Sadder than sorrow, sweeter than delight,
That burthens now the breath of everything,
Though each one sighs as if to each alone
The cherish'd pang were known ?

At dusk of dawn, on his dark spray apart,
With it the Blackbird breaks the young Day's
    heart;
In evening's hush
About it talks the heavenly-minded Thrush;
The hill with like remorse
Smiles to the Sun's smile in his westering course;
The fisher's drooping skiff
In yonder sheltering bay;
The choughs that call about the shining cliff:
The children, noisy in the setting ray;
Own the sweet season, each thing as it may;
Thoughts of strange kindness and forgotten peace
In me increase;
And tears arise
Within my happy, happy Mistress' eyes,
And, lo, her lips, averted from my kiss,
Ask for Love's bounty, ah, much more than bliss:
  Is't the sequester'd and exceeding sweet
Of dear Desire electing his defeat?
Is't the waked Earth now to yon purpling cope
Uttering first-love's first cry,
Vainly renouncing, with a Seraph's sigh,
Love's natural hope?
Fair-meaning Earth, foredoom'd to perjury!
Behold, all-amorous May,

SAINT VALENTINE'S DAY

With roses heap'd upon her laughing brows,
Avoids thee of thy vows !
Were it for thee, with her warm bosom near,
To abide the sharpness of the Seraph's sphere ?
Forget thy foolish words ;
Go to her summons gay,
Thy heart with dead, wing'd Innocencies fill'd.
Ev'n as a nest with birds
After the old ones by the hawk are kill'd.
    Well dost thou, Love, to celebrate
The noon of thy soft ecstasy,
Or e'er it be too late,
Or e'er the Snowdrop die !

.

THE WED-
DING SERMON

THE truths of Love are like the sea
For clearness and for mystery.
Of that sweet love which, startling, wakes
Maiden and Youth, and mostly breaks
The word of promise to the ear,
But keeps it, after many a year,
To the full spirit, how shall I speak ?
My memory with age is weak,
And I for hopes do oft suspect
The things I seem to recollect.
Yet who but must remember well
'Twas this made heaven intelligible
As motive, though 'twas small the power
The heart might have, for even an hour,
To hold possession of the height
Of nameless pathos and delight !

THE PARAGON

When I behold the skies aloft
   Passing the pageantry of dreams,
The cloud whose bosom, cygnet-soft,
   A couch for nuptial Juno seems,
The ocean broad, the mountains bright,
   The shadowy vales with feeding herds,
I from my lyre the music smite,
   Nor want for justly matching words.
All forces of the sea and air,
   All interests of hill and plain,
I so can sing, in seasons fair,
   That who hath felt may feel again.
Elated oft by such free songs,
   I think with utterance free to raise
That hymn for which the whole world longs,
   A worthy hymn in woman's praise ;
A hymn bright-noted like a bird's,
   Arousing these song-sleepy times

With rhapsodies of perfect words,
  Ruled by returning kiss of rhymes.
But when I look on her and hope
  To tell with joy what I admire,
My thoughts lie cramp'd in narrow scope,
  Or in the feeble birth expire ;
No mystery of well-woven speech,
  No simplest phrase of tenderest fall,
No liken'd excellence can reach
  Her, the most excellent of all,
The best half of creation's best,
  Its heart to feel, its eye to see,
The crown and complex of the rest,
  Its aim and its epitome.
Nay, might I utter my conceit,
  'Twere after all a vulgar song,
For she's so simply, subtly sweet,
  My deepest rapture does her wrong.

THE ROSE OF
THE WORLD

Lo, when the Lord made North and South,
   And sun and moon ordained, He,
Forthbringing each by word of mouth
   In order of its dignity,
Did man from the crude clay express
   By sequence, and, all else decreed,
He form'd the woman ; nor might less
   Than Sabbath such a work succeed.
And still with favour singled out,
   Marr'd less than man by mortal fall,
Her disposition is devout,
   Her countenance angelical ;
The best things that the best believe
   Are in her face so kindly writ
The faithless, seeing her, conceive
   Not only heaven, but hope of it ;
No idle thought her instinct shrouds,
   But fancy chequers settled sense,
Like alteration of the clouds

On noonday's azure permanence ;
Pure dignity, composure, ease
   Declare affections nobly fix'd,
And impulse sprung from due degrees
   Of sense and spirit sweetly mix'd.
Her modesty, her chiefest grace,
   The cestus clasping Venus' side,
How potent to deject the face
   Of him who would affront its pride !
Wrong dares not in her presence speak,
   Nor spotted thought its taint disclose
Under the protest of a cheek
   Outbragging Nature's boast the rose.
In mind and manners how discreet ;
   How artless in her very art ;
How candid in discourse ; how sweet
   The concord of her lips and heart ;
How simple and how circumspect ;
   How subtle and how fancy-free ;
Though sacred to her love, how deck'd
   With unexclusive courtesy ;
How quick in talk to see from far
   The way to vanquish or evade ;
How able her persuasions are
   To prove, her reasons to persuade ;
How (not to call true instinct's bent

And woman's very nature, harm),
How amiable and innocent
    Her pleasure in her power to charm ;
How humbly careful to attract,
    Though crown'd with all the soul desires,
Connubial aptitude exact,
    Diversity that never tires.

THE LOVER

He meets, by heavenly chance express,
   The destined maid ; some hidden hand
Unveils to him that loveliness
   Which others cannot understand.
His merits in her presence grow,
   To match the promise in her eyes,
And round her happy footsteps blow
   The authentic airs of Paradise.
For joy of her he cannot sleep ;
   Her beauty haunts him all the night :
It melts his heart, it makes him weep
   For wonder, worship, and delight.
O, paradox of love, he longs,
   Most humble when he most aspires,
To suffer scorn and cruel wrongs
   From her he honours and desires.
Her graces make him rich, and ask
   No guerdon ; this imperial style
Affronts him ; he disdains to bask,

The pensioner of her priceless smile.
He prays for some hard thing to do,
　　Some work of fame and labour immense,
To stretch the languid bulk and thew
　　Of love's fresh-born magnipotence.
No smallest boon were bought too dear,
　　Though barter'd for his love-sick life ;
Yet trusts he, with undaunted cheer,
　　To vanquish heaven, and call her Wife.
He notes how queens of sweetness still
　　Neglect their crowns, and stoop to mate ;
How, self-consign'd with lavish will,
　　They ask but love proportionate ;
How swift pursuit by small degrees,
　　Love's tactic, works like miracle ;
How valour, clothed in courtesies,
　　Brings down the haughtiest citadel ;
And therefore, though he merits not
　　To kiss the braid upon her skirt,
His hope, discouraged ne'er a jot,
　　Out-soars all possible desert.

HEAVEN AND EARTH

How long shall men deny the flower
   Because its roots are in the earth,
And crave with tears from God the dower
   They have, and have despised as dearth,
And scorn as low their human lot,
   With frantic pride, too blind to see
That standing on the head makes not
   Either for ease or dignity !
But fools shall feel like fools to find
   (Too late inform'd) that angels' mirth
Is one in cause, and mode, and kind
   With that which they profaned on earth.

THE LETTER

'O, MORE than dear, be more than just,
   'And do not deafly shut the door !
'I claim no right to speak ; I trust
   'Mercy, not right ; yet who has more ?
'For, if more love makes not more fit,
   'Of claimants here none's more nor less,
'Since your great worth does not permit
   'Degrees in our unworthiness.
'Yet, if there's aught that can be done
   'With arduous labour of long years,
'By which you'll say that you'll be won,
   'O tell me, and I'll dry my tears.
'Ah, no ; if loving cannot move,
   'How foolishly must labour fail !
'The use of deeds is to show love ;
   'If signs suffice let these avail :
'Your name pronounced brings to my heart
   'A feeling like the violet's breath,
'Which does so much of heaven impart

' It makes me amorous of death ;
' The winds that in the garden toss
  ' The Guelder-roses give me pain,
' Alarm me with the dread of loss,
  ' Exhaust me with the dream of gain ;
' I'm troubled by the clouds that move ;
  ' Tired by the breath which I respire ;
' And ever, like a torch, my love,
  ' Thus agitated, flames the higher ;
' All's hard that has not you for goal ;
  ' I scarce can move my hand to write,
' For love engages all my soul,
  ' And leaves the body void of might ;
' The wings of will spread idly, as do
  ' The bird's that in a vacuum lies ;
' My breast, asleep with dreams of you,
  ' Forgets to breathe, and bursts in sighs ;
' I see no rest this side the grave,
  ' No rest nor hope, from you apart ;
' Your life is in the rose you gave,
  ' Its perfume suffocates my heart ;
' There's no refreshment in the breeze ;
  ' The heaven o'erwhelms me with its blue ;
' I faint beside the dancing seas ;
  ' Winds, skies, and waves are only you ;
' The thought or act which not intends

'You service, seems a sin and shame ;
'In that one only object ends
  'Conscience, religion, honour, fame.
'Ah, could I put off love ! Could we
  'Never have met ! What calm, what ease !
'Nay, but, alas, this remedy
  'Were ten times worse than the disease !
'For when, indifferent, I pursue
  'The world's best pleasures for relief,
'My heart, still sickening back to you,
  'Finds none like memory of its grief ;
'And, though 'twere very hell to hear
  'You felt such misery as I,
'All good, save you, were far less dear
  'Than is that ill with which I die !
'Where'er I go, wandering forlorn,
  'You are the world's love, life, and glee :
'Oh, wretchedness not to be borne
  'If she that's Love should not love me !'

THE REVE-
LATION

An idle poet, here and there,
  Looks round him; but, for all the rest,
The world, unfathomably fair,
  Is duller than a witling's jest.
Love wakes men, once a lifetime each;
  They lift their heavy lids, and look;
And, lo, what one sweet page can teach,
  They read with joy, then shut the book.
And some give thanks, and some blaspheme,
  And most forget; but, either way,
That and the Child's unheeded dream
  Is all the light of all their day

THE DOUBT

THE moods of love are like the wind,
    And none knows whence or why they rise :
I ne'er before felt heart and mind
    So much affected through mine eyes.
How cognate with the flatter'd air,
    How form'd for earth's familiar zone,
She moved ; how feeling and how fair
    For others' pleasure and her own !
And, ah, the heaven of her face !
    How, when she laugh'd I seem'd to see
The gladness of the primal grace,
    And how, when grave, its dignity !
Of all she was, the least not less
    Delighted the devoted eye ;
No fold or fashion of her dress
    Her fairness did not sanctify.
I could not else than grieve. What cause ?
    Was I not blest ? Was she not there ?
Likely my own ? Ah, that it was :
    How like seem'd 'likely' to despair !

SECURITY

But as we talk'd, my spirit quaff'd
  The sparkling winds ; the candid skies
At our untruthful strangeness laugh'd :
  I kiss'd with mine her smiling eyes ;
And sweet familiarness and awe
  Prevail'd that hour on either part,
And in the eternal light I saw
  That she was mine ; though yet my heart
Could not conceive, nor would confess
  Such contentation ; and there grew
More form and more fair stateliness
  Than heretofore between us two.

THE SPIRIT'S EPOCHS

Not in the crises of events,
  Of compass'd hopes, or fears fulfill'd,
Or acts of gravest consequence,
  Are life's delight and depth reveal'd.
The day of days was not the day;
  That went before, or was postponed;
The night Death took our lamp away
  Was not the night on which we groan'd.
I drew my bride, beneath the moon,
  Across my threshold; happy hour!
But, ah, the walk that afternoon
  We saw the water-flags in flower!

THE MAID

SHE wearies with an ill unknown;
  In sleep she sobs and seems to float,
A water-lily, all alone
  Within a lonely castle moat
And as the full-moon, spectral, lies
  Within the crescent's gleaming arms,
The present shows her heedless eyes
  A future dim with vague alarms.
She sees, and yet she scarcely sees,
  For, life-in-life not yet begun,
Too many are its mysteries
  For thought to fix on any one.

ACCEPTANCE

Twice rose, twice died my trembling word ;
  The faint and frail Cathedral chimes
Spake time in music, and we heard
  The chafers rustling in the limes.
Her dress, that touch'd me where I stood,
  The warmth of her confided arm,
Her bosom's gentle neighbourhood,
  Her pleasure in her power to charm ;
Her look, her love, her form, her touch,
  The least seem'd most by blissful turn,
Blissful but that it pleased too much,
  And taught the wayward soul to yearn.
It was as if a harp with wires
  Was traversed by the breath I drew ;
And oh, sweet meeting of desires,
  She, answering, own'd that she loved too.

BETROTHED

What fortune did my heart foretell?
　　What shook my spirit, as I woke,
Like the vibration of a bell
　　Of which I had not heard the stroke?
Was it some happy vision shut
　　From memory by the sun's fresh ray?
Was it that linnet's song; or but
　　A natural gratitude for day?
Or the mere joy the senses weave,
　　A wayward ecstasy of life?
Then I remember'd, yester-eve
　　I won Honoria for my Wife.

THE DANCE

But there danced she, who from the leaven
    Of ill preserv'd my heart and wit
All unawares, for she was heaven,
    Others at best but fit for it.
One of those lovely things she was
    In whose least action there can be
Nothing so transient but it has
    An air of immortality.
I mark'd her step, with peace elate,
    Her brow more beautiful than morn,
Her sometime look of girlish state
    Which sweetly waived its right to scorn
The giddy crowd, she grave the while,
    Although, as 'twere beyond her will,
Around her mouth the baby smile,
    That she was born with, linger'd still.
Her ball-dress seem'd a breathing mist,
    From the fair form exhaled and shed,
Raised in the dance with arm and wrist

All warmth and light, unbraceleted.
Her motion, feeling 'twas beloved,
   The pensive soul of tune express'd,
And, oh, what perfume, as she moved,
   Came from the flowers in her breast !
Ah, none but I discern'd her looks,
   When in the throng she pass'd me by,
For love is like a ghost, and brooks
   Only the chosen seer's eye ;
And who but she could e'er divine
   The halo and the happy trance,
When her bright arm reposed on mine,
   In all the pauses of the dance !

ENTREATY

'O Dearest, tell me how to prove
  'Goodwill which cannot be express'd ;
'The beneficial heart of love
  'Is labour in an idle breast.'

THE REVULSION

'Twas when the spousal time of May
  Hangs all the hedge with bridal wreaths,
And air's so sweet the bosom gay
  Gives thanks for every breath it breathes;
When like to like is gladly moved,
  And each thing joins in Spring's refrain,
' Let those love now who never loved ;
  ' Let those who have loved love again ; '
That I, in whom the sweet time wrought,
  Lay stretch'd within a lonely glade,
Abandon'd to delicious thought,
  Beneath the softly twinkling shade.

And so I mused, till musing brought
  A dream that shook my house of clay,
And, in my humbled heart, I thought,
  To me there yet may come a day
With this the single vestige seen
  Of comfort, earthly or divine,

THE REVULSION

My sorrow some time must have been
 Her portion, had it not been mine.
Then I, who knew, from watching life,
 That blows foreseen are slow to fall,
Rehearsed the losing of a wife,
 And faced its terrors each and all.
The self-chastising fancy show'd
 The coffin with its ghastly breath :
The innocent sweet face that owed
 None of its innocence to death ;
The lips that used to laugh ; the knell
 That bade the world beware of mirth ;
The heartless and intolerable
 Indignity of ' earth to earth ;'
At morn remembering by degrees
 That she I dream'd about was dead ;
Love's still recurrent jubilees,
 The days that she was born, won, wed';
The duties of my life the same,
 Their meaning for the feelings gone ;
Friendship impertinent, and fame
 Disgusting ; and, more harrowing none,
Small household troubles fall'n to me,
 As, ' What time would I dine to-day ? '
And, oh, how could I bear to see
 The noisy children at their play.

Besides, where all things limp and halt,
    Could I go straight, should I alone
Have kept my love without default
    Pitch'd at the true and heavenly tone ?
The festal-day might come to mind
    That miss'd the gift which more endears ;
The hour which might have been more kind,
    And now less fertile in vain tears ;
The good of common intercourse,
    For daintier pleasures then despised,
Now with what passionate remorse,
    What poignancy of hunger prized !
The little wrong, now greatly rued,
    Which no repentance now could right ;
And love, in disbelieving mood,
    Deserting his celestial height.
Withal to know, God's love sent grief
    To make me less the world's, and more
Meek-hearted : ah, the sick relief !
    Why bow'd I not my heart before ?

PRAISES

I PRAISED her, but no praise could fill
 The depths of her desire to please,
Though dull to others as a Will
 To them that have no legacies.
The more I praised the more she shone,
 Her eyes incredulously bright,
And all her happy beauty blown
 Beneath the beams of my delight.
Sweet rivalry was thus begot ;
 By turns, my speech, in passion's style,
With flatteries the truth o'ershot,
 And she surpass'd them with her smile.

' Nature to you was more than kind ;
 ' 'Twas fond perversity to dress
' So much simplicity of mind
 ' In such a pomp of loveliness !

MARRIAGE

Forth, from the glittering spirit's peace
    And gaiety ineffable,
Stream'd to the heart delight and ease,
    As from an overflowing well;
And, orderly deriving thence
    Its pleasure perfect and allow'd.
Bright with the spirit shone the sense,
    As with the sun a fleecy cloud.

THE ROSY BOSOM'D
HOURS

A FLORIN to the willing Guard
   Secured, for half the way,
(He lock'd us in, ah, lucky-starr'd,)
   A curtain'd, front coupé.
The sparkling sun of August shone;
   The wind was in the West;
Your gown and all that you had on
   Was what became you best;
And we were in that seldom mood
   When soul with soul agrees,
Mingling, like flood with equal flood,
   In agitated ease.
Far round, each blade of harvest bare
   Its little load of bread;
Each furlong of that journey fair
   With separate sweetness sped.
The calm of use was coming o'er
   The wonder of our wealth,
And now, maybe, 'twas not much more

Than Eden's common health.
We paced the sunny platform, while
    The train at Havant changed :
What made the people kindly smile,
    Or stare with looks estranged ?
Too radiant for a wife you seem'd,
    Serener than a bride ;
Me happiest born of men I deem'd,
    And show'd perchance my pride.
I loved that girl, so gaunt and tall,
    Who whispered loud, 'Sweet Thing !'
Scanning your figure, slight yet all
    Round as your own gold ring.
At Salisbury you stray'd alone
    Within the shafted glooms,
Whilst I was by the Verger shown
    The brasses and the tombs.
At tea we talk'd of matters deep,
    Of joy that never dies ;
We laugh'd, till love was mix'd with sleep
    Within your great sweet eyes.
The next day, sweet with luck no less
    And sense of sweetness past,
The full tide of our happiness
    Rose higher than the last.
At Dawlish, 'mid the pools of brine,

THE ROSY BOSOM'D HOURS

You stept from rock to rock,
One hand quick tightening upon mine,
One holding up your frock.
On starfish and on weeds alone
You seem'd intent to be :
Flash'd those great gleams of hope unknown
From you, or from the sea?
Ne'er came before, ah, when again
Shall come two days like these :
Such quick delight within the brain,
Within the heart such peace?
I thought, indeed, by magic chance,
A third from Heaven to win,
But as, at dusk, we reach'd Penzance,
A drizzling rain set in.

WIND AND WAVE

THE wedded light and heat,
Winnowing the witless space,
Without a let,
What are they till they beat
Against the sleepy sod, and there beget
Perchance the violet !
Is the One found,
Amongst a wilderness of as happy grace,
To make Heaven's bound ;
So that in Her
All which it hath of sensitively good
Is sought and understood
After the narrow mode the mighty Heavens
        prefer ?
She, as a little breeze
Following still Night,
Ripples the spirit's cold, deep seas
Into delight ;
But, in a while,

WIND AND WAVE

The immeasurable smile
Is broke by fresher airs to flashes blent
With darkling discontent :
And all the subtle zephyr hurries gay,
And all the heaving ocean heaves one way,
T'ward the void sky-line and an unguess'd weal .
Until the vanward billows feel
The agitating shallows, and divine the goal,
And to foam roll,
And spread and stray
And traverse wildly, like delighted hands,
The fair and fleckless sands ;
And so the whole
Unfathomable and immense
Triumphing tide comes at the last to reach
And burst in wind-kiss'd splendours on the deaf-
    'ning beach,
Where forms of children in first innocence
Laugh and fling pebbles on the rainbow'd crest
Of its untired unrest.

BEATA

OF infinite Heaven the rays,
Piercing some eyelet in our cavern black,
Ended their viewless track
On thee to smite
Solely, as on a diamond stalactite,
And in mid-darkness lit a rainbow's blaze,
Wherein the absolute Reason, Power, and Love,
That erst could move
Mainly in me but toil and weariness,
Renounced their deadening might,
Renounced their undistinguishable stress
Of withering white,
And did with gladdest hues my spirit caress,
Nothing of Heaven in thee showing infinite,
Save the delight.

IF I WERE DEAD

' IF I were dead, you'd sometimes say, Poor
    Child ! '
The dear lips quiver'd as they spake,
And the tears brake
From eyes which, not to grieve me, brightly smiled.
Poor Child, poor Child !
I seem to hear your laugh, your talk, your song.
It is not true that Love will do no wrong.
Poor Child !
And did you think, when you so cried and smiled,
How I, in lonely nights, should lie awake,
And of those words your full avengers make ?
Poor Child, poor Child !
And now, unless it be
That sweet amends thrice told are come to thee.
O God, have Thou *no* mercy upon me !
Poor Child !

DELICIÆ SAPIENTIÆ
DE AMORE

Love, light for me
Thy ruddiest blazing torch,
That I, albeit a beggar by the Porch
Of the glad Palace of Virginity,
May gaze within, and sing the pomp I see;
For, crown'd with roses all,
'Tis there, O Love, they keep thy festival!
But first warn off the beatific spot
Those wretched who have not
Even afar beheld the shining wall,
And those who, once beholding, have forgot,
And those, most vile, who dress
The charnel spectre drear
Of utterly dishallow'd nothingness
In that refulgent fame,
And cry, Lo, here!
And name
The Lady whose smiles inflame
The sphere.

DELICIÆ SAPIENTIÆ DE AMORE

Bring, Love, anear,
And bid be not afraid
Young Lover true, and Love-foreboding Maid,
And wedded Spouse, if virginal of thought ;
For I will sing of nought
Less sweet to hear
Than seems
A music in their half-remember'd dreams.
  The magnet calls the steel :
Answers the iron to the magnet's breath ;
What do they feel
But death !
The clouds of summer kiss in flame and rain,
And are not found again ;
But the heavens themselves eternal are with fire
Of unapproach'd desire,
By the aching heart of Love, which cannot rest,
In blissfullest pathos so indeed possess'd.
O, spousals high ;
O, doctrine blest,
Unutterable in even the happiest sigh ;
This know ye all
Who can recall
With what a welling of indignant tears
Love's simpleness first hears
The meaning of his mortal covenant,

And from what pride comes down
To wear the crown
Of which 'twas very heaven to feel the want.
How envies he the ways
Of yonder hopeless star,
And so would laugh and yearn
With trembling lids eterne,
Ineffably content from infinitely far
Only to gaze
On his bright Mistress's responding rays,
That never know eclipse;
And, once in his long year,
With præternuptial ecstasy and fear,
By the delicious law of that ellipse
Wherein all citizens of ether move,
With hastening pace to come
Nearer, though never near,
His Love
And always inaccessible sweet Home;
There on his path doubly to burn,
Kiss'd by her doubled light
That whispers of its source,
The ardent secret ever clothed with Night,
Then go forth in new force
Towards a new return,
Rejoicing as a Bridegroom on his course !

DELICIÆ SAPIENTIÆ DE AMORE

This know ye all;
Therefore gaze bold,
That so in you be joyful hope increas'd,
Thorough the Palace portals, and behold
The dainty and unsating Marriage-Feast.
O, hear
Them singing clear
' Cor meum et caro mea' round the ' I am,'
The Husband of the Heavens, and the Lamb
Whom they for ever follow there that kept,
Or losing, never slept
Till they reconquer'd had in mortal fight
The standard white.
O, hear
From the harps they bore from Earth, five-strung,
    what music springs,
While the glad Spirits chide
The wondering strings !
And how the shining sacrificial Choirs,
Offering for aye their dearest hearts' desires,
Which to their hearts come back beatified,
Hymn, the bright aisles along,
The nuptial song,
Song ever new to us and them, that saith,
' Hail Virgin in Virginity a Spouse ! '
Heard first below

DELICIÆ SAPIENTIÆ DE AMORE

Within the little house
At Nazareth ;
Heard yet in many a cell where brides of Christ
Lie hid, emparadised,
And where, although
By the hour 'tis night,
There's light,
The Day still lingering in the lap of snow.
Gaze and be not afraid
Ye wedded few that honour, in sweet thought
And glittering will,
So freshly from the garden gather still
The lily sacrificed ;
For ye, though self-suspected here for nought,
Are highly styled
With the thousands twelve times twelve of unde-
    filed.
Gaze and be not afraid
Young Lover true and love-foreboding Maid.
The full noon of deific vision bright
Abashes nor abates
No spark minute of Nature's keen delight.
'Tis there your Hymen waits !
There where in courts afar, all unconfused, they
    crowd,
As fumes the starlight soft

53

DELICIÆ SAPIENTIÆ DE AMORE

In gulfs of cloud,
And each to the other, well-content,
Sighs oft,
'"Twas this we meant!'
Gaze without blame
Ye in whom living Love yet blushes for dead
    shame.
There of pure Virgins none
Is fairer seen,
Save One,
Than Mary Magdalene.
Gaze without doubt or fear
Ye to whom generous Love, by any name, is dear
Love makes the life to be
A fount perpetual of virginity;
For, lo, the Elect
Of generous Love, how nam'd soe'er, affect
Nothing but God,
Or mediate or direct,
Nothing but God,
The Husband of the Heavens:
And who Him love, in potence great or small,
Are, one and all,
Heirs of the Palace glad,
And inly clad
With the bridal robes of ardour virginal.

MIGNONNE

WHATE'ER thou dost thou'rt dear.
Uncertain troubles sanctify
That magic well-spring of the willing tear,
Thine eye.
Thy jealous fear,
With not the rustle of a rival near ;
Thy careless disregard of all
My tenderest care ;
Thy dumb despair
When thy keen wit my worship may construe
Into contempt of thy divinity ;
They please me too !
But should it once befall
These accidental charms to disappear,
Leaving withal
Thy sometime self the same throughout the year,
So glowing, grave and shy,
Kind, talkative and dear
As now thou sitt'st to ply

MIGNONNE

The fireside tune
Of that neat engine deft at which thou sew'st
With fingers mild and foot like the new moon,
O, then what cross of any further fate
Could my content abate?
Forget, then, (but I know
Thou canst not so,)
Thy customs of some prædiluvian state.
I am no Bullfinch, fair my Butterfly,
That thou should'st try
Those zigzag courses, in the welkin clear;
Nor cruel Boy that, fledd'st thou straight
Or paused, mayhap
Might catch thee, for thy colours, with his cap.

MILDRED

Mildred's of Earth, yet happier far
Than most men's thoughts of Heaven are.

REJECTED

'Perhaps she's dancing somewhere now!'
    The thoughts of light and music wake
Sharp jealousies, that grow and grow
    Till silence and the darkness ache.
He sees her step, so proud and gay,
    Which, ere he spake, foretold despair;
Thus did she look, on such a day,
    And such the fashion of her hair;
And thus she stood, when, kneeling low,
    He took the bramble from her dress,
And thus she laugh'd and talk'd, whose 'No'
    Was sweeter than another's 'Yes.'
He feeds on thoughts that most deject;
    He impudently feigns her charms,
So reverenced in his own respect,
    Dreadfully clasp'd by other arms;
And turns, and puts his brows, that ache,
    Against the pillow where 'tis cold.
If only now his heart would break!
    But, oh, how much a heart can hold.

LOVE IN TEARS

If fate Love's dear ambition mar,
   And load his breast with hopeless pain,
And seem to blot out sun and star,
   Love, won or lost, is countless gain ;
His sorrow boasts a secret bliss
   Which sorrow of itself beguiles,
And Love in tears too noble is
   For pity, save of Love in smiles.

DENIED

The storm-cloud, whose portentous shade
    Fumes from a core of smother'd fire,
His livery is whose worshipp'd maid
    Denies herself to his desire.
Ah, grief that almost crushes life,
    To lie upon his lonely bed,
And fancy her another's wife !
    His brain is flame, his heart is lead.
Sinking at last, by nature's course,
    Cloak'd round with sleep from his despair,
He does but sleep to gather force
    That goes to his exhausted care.
He wakes renew'd for all the smart.
    His only Love, and she is wed !
His fondness comes about his heart,
    As milk comes, when the babe is dead.
The wretch, whom she found fit for scorn,
    His own allegiant thoughts despise ;
And far into the shining morn
    Lazy with misery he lies.

LOVE'S WILL
BE DONE

Not loss, not death, my love shall tire.
A mystery does my heart foretell ;
Nor do I press the oracle
For explanations.   Leave me alone,
And let in me love's will be done.

FIRST LOVE
REMEMBERED

As, ere the Spring has any power,
The almond branch all turns to flower,
Though not a leaf is out, so she
The bloom of life provoked in me ;
And, hard till then and selfish, I
Was thenceforth nought but sanctity
And service : life was mere delight
In being wholly good and right,
As she was ; just, without a slur ;
Honouring myself no less than her ;
Obeying, in the loneliest place,
Ev'n to the slightest gesture, grace,
Assured that one so fair, so true,
He only served that was so too.
For me, hence weak towards the weak,
No more the unnested blackbird's shriek
Startled the light-leaved wood ; on high
Wander'd the gadding butterfly,
Unscared by my flung cap ; the bee,

FIRST LOVE REMEMBERED

Rifling the hollyhock in glee,
Was no more trapp'd with his own flower,
And for his honey slain.   Her power,
From great things even to the grass
Through which the unfenced footways pass,
Was law, and that which keeps the law,
Cherubic gaiety and awe ;
Day was her doing, and the lark
Had reason for his song ; the dark
In anagram innumerous spelt
Her name with stars that throbb'd and felt ;
'Twas the sad summit of delight
To wake and weep for her at night ;
She turn'd to triumph or to shame
The strife of every childish game ;
The heart would come into my throat
At rosebuds ; howsoe'er remote,
In opposition or consent,
Each thing, or person, or event,
Or seeming neutral howsoe'er,
All, in the live, electric air,
Awoke, took aspect, and confess'd
In her a centre of unrest,
Yea, stocks and stones within me bred
Anxieties of joy and dread.
    O, bright apocalyptic sky

FIRST LOVE REMEMBERED

O'erarching childhood ! Far and nigh
Mystery and obscuration none,
Yet nowhere any moon or sun !
What reason for these sighs ? What hope,
Daunting with its audacious scope
The disconcerted heart, affects
These ceremonies and respects ?
Why stratagems in everything ?
Why, why not kiss her in the ring ?
'Tis nothing strange that warriors bold,
Whose fierce, forecasting eyes behold
The city they desire to sack,
Humbly begin their proud attack
By delving ditches two miles off,
Aware how the fair place would scoff
At hasty wooing ; but, O child,
Why thus approach thy playmate mild ?

LOST LOVE

Fashion'd by Heaven and by art
So is she, that she makes the heart
Ache and o'erflow with tears, that grace
So lovely fair should have for place,
(Deeming itself at home the while,)
The unworthy earth !   To see her smile
Amid this waste of pain and sin,
As only knowing the heaven within,
Is sweet, and does for pity stir
Passion to be her minister :
Wherefore last night I lay awake,
And said, ' Ah, Lord, for thy love's sake,
Give not this darling child of thine
To care less reverent than mine ! '
And, as true faith was in my word,
I trust, I trust that I was heard.

AWAY

The multitude of voices blythe
Of early day, the hissing scythe
Across the dew drawn and withdrawn,
The noisy peacock on the lawn,
These, and the sun's eye-gladding gleam,
This morning, chased the sweetest dream
That e'er shed penitential grace
On life's forgetful commonplace ;
Yet 'twas no sweeter than the spell
To which I woke to say farewell.
Noon finds me many a mile removed
From her who must not be beloved ;
And us the waste sea soon shall part,
Heaving for aye, without a heart !

   Beholding one like her, a man
Longs to lay down his life ! How can
Aught to itself seem thus enough
When I have so much need thereof ?

Blest in her place, blissful is she;
And I, departing, seem to be
Like the strange waif that comes to run
A few days flaming near the sun,
And carries back, through boundless night,
Its lessening memory of light.

Had I but her, ah, what the gain
Of owning aught but that domain!
Nay, heaven's extent, however much,
Cannot be more than many such;
And, she being mine, should God to me
Say 'Lo! my Child, I give to thee
All heaven besides,' what could I then,
But, as a child, to Him complain
That whereas my dear Father gave
A little space for me to have
In His great garden, now, o'erblest,
I've that, indeed, but all the rest,
Which, somehow, makes it seem I've
    got
All but my only cared-for plot.
Enough was that for my weak hand
To tend, my heart to understand.
Oh, the sick fact, 'twixt her and me
There's naught, and half a world of sea.

Yet, latterly, with strange delight,
Rich tides have risen in the night,
And sweet dreams chased the fancies dense
Of waking life's dull somnolence.
I see her as I knew her, grace
Already glory in her face ;
I move about, I cannot rest, '
For the proud brain and joyful breast
I have of her.   Or else I float,
The pilot of an idle boat,
Alone, alone with sky and sea,
And her, the third simplicity.
Or with me, in the Ball-Room's blaze,
Her brilliant mildness thrids the maze ;
Our thoughts are lovely, and each word
Is music in the music heard,
And all things seem but parts to be
Of one persistent harmony,
By which I'm made divinely bold ;
The secret, which she knows, is told :
And, laughing with a lofty bliss
Of innocent accord, we kiss ;
About her neck my pleasure weeps ;
Against my lip the silk vein leaps ;
Then says an Angel, ' Day or night,
' If yours you seek, not her delight,

' Although by some strange witchery
' It seems you kiss her, 'tis not she ;
' But, whilst you languish at the side
' Of a fair-foul phantasmal bride,
'Surely a dragon and strong tower
' Guard the true lady in her bower.'
And I say, 'Dear my Lord, Amen !'
And the true lady kiss again.
Or else some wasteful malady
Devours her shape and dims her eye ;
No charms are left, where all were rife,
Except her voice, which is her life,
Wherewith she, for her foolish fear,
Says trembling, ' Do you love me, Dear ? '
And I reply, 'Sweetest, I vow
' I never loved but half till now.'
She turns her face to the wall at this,
And says, ' Go, Love, 'tis too much bliss.'
And then a sudden pulse is sent
About the sounding firmament
In smitings as of silver bars ;
The bright disorder of the stars
Is solved by music ; far and near,
Through infinite distinctions clear,
Their twofold voices' deeper tone
Utters the Name which all things own,

And each ecstatic treble dwells
On one whereof none other tells ;
And we, sublimed to song and fire,
Take order in the wheeling quire,
Till from the throbbing sphere I start,
Waked by the heaving of my heart.

There comes a smile acutely sweet
Out of the picturing dark ; I meet
The ancient frankness of her gaze,
That soft and heart-surprising blaze
Of great goodwill and innocence,
And perfect joy proceeding thence !
Ah ! made for earth's delight, yet such
The mid-sea air's too gross to touch.
At thought of which, the soul in me
Is as the bird that bites a bee,
And darts abroad on frantic wing,
Tasting the honey and the sting.

I grew so idle, so despised
Myself, my powers, by Her unprized,
Honouring my post, but nothing more,
And lying, when I lived on shore,
So late of mornings : weak tears stream'd,
For such slight cause,—if only gleam'd,

Remotely, beautifully bright,
On clouded eves at sea, the light
Of English headlands in the sun,—
That soon I deem'd 'twere better done
To lay this poor, complaining wraith
Of unreciprocated faith.

RACHEL

You loved her, and would lie all night
    Thinking how beautiful she was,
And what to do for her delight.
    Now both are bound with alien laws!
Be patient; put your heart to school;
    Weep if you will, but not despair;
The trust that nought goes wrong by rule
    Should ease this load the many bear.
Love, if there's heav'n, shall meet his dues,
    Though here unmatch'd, or match'd amiss;
Meanwhile, the gentle cannot choose
    But learn to love the lips they kiss.
Ne'er hurt the homely sister's ears
    With Rachel's beauties; secret be
The lofty mind whose lonely tears
    Protest against mortality.

THE VOICE OF
ONE I KNEW

ALL the bright past seems,
Now, but a splendour in my dreams,
Which shows, albeit the dreamer wakes,
The standard of right life.   Life aches
To be therewith conform'd ; but, oh,
The world's so stolid, dark, and low !
That and the mortal element
Forbid the beautiful intent,
And, like the unborn butterfly,
It feels the wings, and wants the sky.
But perilous is the lofty mood
Which cannot yoke with lowly good
Right life, for me, is life that wends
By lowly ways to lofty ends.
I well perceive, at length, that haste
T'ward heaven itself is only waste ;
And thus I dread the impatient spur
Of aught that speaks too plain of Her
There's little here that story tells ;

But music talks of nothing else.
Therefore, when music breathes, I say,
(And urge my task,) Away, away !
Thou art the voice of one I knew,
But what thou say'st is not yet true ;
Thou art the voice of her I loved,
And I would not be vainly moved.

IN THE WOODS

AND then, as if I sweetly dream'd,
I half-remember'd how it seem'd
When I, too, was a little child
About the wild wood roving wild.
Pure breezes from the far-off height
Melted the blindness from my sight,
Until, with rapture, grief, and awe,
I saw again as then I saw.
As then I saw, I saw again
The harvest-waggon in the lane,
With high-hung tokens of its pride
Left in the elms on either side ;
The daisies coming out at dawn
In constellations on the lawn ;
The glory of the daffodil ;
The three black windmills on the hill,
Whose magic arms, flung wildly by,
Sent magic shadows o'er the rye.
Within the leafy coppice, lo,

IN THE WOODS

More wealth than miser's dreams could show,
The blackbird's warm and woolly brood,
Five golden beaks agape for food ;
The Gipsies, all the summer seen
Native as poppies to the Green ;
The winter, with its frosts and thaws
And opulence of hips and haws ;
The lovely marvel of the snow ;
The Tamar, with its altering show
Of gay ships sailing up and down,
Among the fields and by the Town ;
And, dearer far than anything,
Came back the songs you used to sing.
And, as to men's retreating eyes,
Beyond high mountains higher rise,
Still farther back there shone to me
The dazzling dusk of infancy.
Thither I look'd, as, sick of night,
The Alpine shepherd looks to the height,
And does not see the day, 'tis true,
But sees the rosy tops that do.

Debtor to few, forgotten hours
Am I, that truths for me are powers.
Ah, happy hours, 'tis something yet
Not to forget that I forget !

LEAH

YOUR love lacks joy, your letter says.
Yes ; love requires the focal space
Of recollection or of hope,
E'er it can measure its own scope.
Too soon, too soon comes Death to show
We love more deeply than we know !
The rain, that fell upon the height
Too gently to be call'd delight,
Within the dark veil reappears
As a wild cataract of tears ;
And love in life should strive to see
Sometimes what love in death would be !

No magic of her voice or smile
Suddenly raised a fairy isle,
But fondness for her underwent
An unregarded increment,
Like that which lifts, through centuries,
The coral-reef within the seas,
Till, lo ! the land where was the wave.
Alas ! 'tis everywhere her grave.

HER COUNSEL.

Oh, should the mournful honeymoon
Of death be over strangely soon,
And life-long resolutions, made
In grievous haste, as quickly fade,
Seeming the truth of grief to mock,
Think, Dearest, 'tis not by the clock
That sorrow goes.   A month of tears
Is more than many, many years
Of common time.   Shun, if you can,
However, any passionate plan.
Grieve with the heart ; let not the head
Grieve on, when grief of heart is dead ;
For all the powers of life defy
A superstitious constancy.

SPONSA DEI

WHAT is this Maiden fair,
The laughing of whose eye
Is in man's heart renew'd virginity;
Who yet sick longing breeds
For marriage which exceeds
The inventive guess of Love to satisfy
With hope of utter binding, and of loosing endless
    dear despair?
What gleams about her shine,
More transient than delight and more divine!
If she does something but a little sweet,
As gaze towards the glass to set her hair,
See how his soul falls humbled at her feet!
Her gentle step, to go or come,
Gains her more merit than a martyrdom;
And, if she dance, it doth such grace confer
As opes the heaven of heavens to more than her,
And makes a rival of her worshipper.
To die unknown for her were little cost!

SPONSA DEI

So is she without guile,
Her mere refused smile
Makes up the sum of that which may be lost !
Who is this Fair
Whom each hath seen,
The darkest once in this bewailed dell,
Be he not destin'd for the glooms of hell ?
Whom each hath seen
And known, with sharp remorse and sweet, as
    Queen
And tear-glad Mistress of his hopes of bliss,
Too fair for man to kiss ?
Who is this only happy She,
Whom, by a frantic flight of courtesy,
Born of despair
Of better lodging for his Spirit fair,
He adores as Margaret, Maude, or Cecily ?
And what this sigh,
That each one heaves for Earth's last lowlihead
And the Heaven high
Ineffably lock'd in dateless bridal-bed ?
Are all, then, mad, or is it prophecy ?
'Sons now we are of God,' as we have heard,
'But what we shall be hath not yet appear'd.'
O, Heart, remember thee,
That Man is none,

Save One.
What if this Lady be thy Soul, and He
Who claims to enjoy her sacred beauty be,
Not Thou, but God ; and thy sick fire
A female vanity,
Such as a Bride, viewing her mirror'd charms,
Feels when she sighs, ' All these are for his arms ! '
A reflex heat
Flash'd on thy cheek from His immense desire,
Which waits to crown, beyond thy brain's conceit,
Thy nameless, secret, hopeless longing sweet,
Not by-and-by, but now,
Unless deny Him thou !

BONDS

For, ah, who can express
How full of bonds and simpleness
Is God,
How narrow is He,
And how the wide, waste field of possibility
Is only trod
Straight to His homestead in the human heart,
And all His art
Is as the babe's that wins his Mother to repeat
Her little song so sweet!

TO THE BODY

CREATION's and Creator's crowning good ;
Wall of infinitude ;
Foundation of the sky,
In Heaven forecast
And long'd for from eternity,
Though laid the last ;
Reverberating dome,
Of music cunningly built home
Against the void and indolent disgrace
Of unresponsive space ;
Little, sequester'd pleasure-house
For God and for His Spouse ;
Elaborately, yea, past conceiving, fair,
Since, from the graced decorum of the hair,
Ev'n to the tingling, sweet
Soles of the simple, earth-confiding feet,
And from the inmost heart
Outwards unto the thin
Silk curtains of the skin,

TO THE BODY

Every least part
Astonish'd hears
And sweet replies to some like region of the
    spheres ;
Form'd for a dignity prophets but darkly name,
Lest shameless men cry 'Shame !'
So rich with wealth conceal'd
That Heaven and Hell fight chiefly for this field ;
Clinging to everything that pleases thee
With indefectible fidelity ;
Alas, so true
To all thy friendships that no grace
Thee from thy sin can wholly disembrace ;
Which thus 'bides with thee as the Jebusite,
That, maugre all God's promises could do,
The chosen People never conquer'd quite ;
Who therefore lived with them,
And that by formal truce and as of right,
In metropolitan Jerusalem.
For which false fealty
Thou needs must, for a season, lie
In the grave's arms, foul and unshriven,
Albeit, in Heaven,
Thy crimson-throbbing Glow
Into its old abode aye pants to go,
And does with envy see

Enoch, Elijah, and the Lady, she
Who left the roses in her body's lieu.
O, if the pleasures I have known in thee
But my poor faith's poor first-fruits be,
What quintessential, keen, ethereal bliss
Then shall be his
Who has thy birth-time's consecrating dew
For death's sweet chrism retain'd,
Quick, tender, virginal, and unprofaned !

AURAS OF DELIGHT

AND Him I thank, who can make live again
The dust, but not the joy we once profane,
That I, of ye,
Beautiful habitations, auras of delight,
In childish years and since had sometime sense
    and sight,
But that ye vanish'd quite,
Even from memory,
Ere I could get my breath, and whisper 'See!'
  But did for me
They altogether die,
Those trackless glories glimps'd in upper sky?
Were they of chance, or vain,
Nor good at all again
For curb of heart or fret?
Nay, though, by grace,
Lest, haply, I refuse God to his face,
Their likeness wholly I forget,
Ah, yet,

Often in straits which else for me were ill,

I mind me still

I *did* respire the lonely auras sweet,

I *did* the blest abodes behold, and, at the mountains' feet,

Bathed in the holy Stream by Hermon's thymy
hill.

PSYCHE

'What awful pleasure do thine eyes bespeak,
What shame is in thy childish cheek,
What terror on thy brow?
Is this my Psyche, once so pale and meek?
      .   .   .   .   .

And all thy life looks troubled like a tree's
Whose boughs wave many ways in one great
      breeze.'

DAWN

'Ah, say not yet, farewell!'
'Nay, that's the Blackbird's note, the sweet
    Night's knell.'
'Thou leav'st me now, like to the moon at dawn,
A little, vacuous world alone in air.'

THE EDGE OF BLISS

' Sadness and change and pain
Shall me for ever stain ;
For, though my blissful fate
Be for a billion years,
How shall I stop my tears
That life was once so low and Love arrived so
     late ! '
  ' Sadness is beauty's savour, and pain is
The exceedingly keen edge of bliss ;
Nor, without swift mutation, would the heav'ns
     be aught.'

EROS

'Accept the sweet, and say 'tis sacrifice!
Sleep, Centre to the tempest of my love,
And dream thereof,
And keep the smile which sleeps within thy face
Like sunny eve in some forgotten place!'

AMELIA

WHENE'ER mine eyes do my Amelia greet
It is with such emotion
As when, in childhood, turning a dim street,
I first beheld the ocean.
  There, where the little, bright, surf-breathing
    town,
That shew'd me first her beauty and the sea,
Gathers its skirts against the gorse-lit down
And scatters gardens o'er the southern lea,
Abides this Maid
Within a kind yet sombre Mother's shade,
Who of her daughter's graces seems almost afraid,
Viewing them ofttimes with a scared forecast,
Caught, haply, from obscure love-peril past.
Howe'er that be,
She scants me of my right,
Is cunning careful evermore to balk
Sweet separate talk,
And fevers my delight

By frets, if, on Amelia's cheek of peach,
I touch the notes which music cannot reach,
Bidding ' Good-night ! '

   .   .   .   .   .

  And there Amelia stood, for fairness shewn
Like a young apple-tree, in flush'd array
Of white and ruddy flow'r, auroral, gay,
With chilly blue the maiden branch between ;
And yet to look on her moved less the mind
To say ' How beauteous ! ' than ' How good and
    kind ! '
  And so we went alone
By walls o'er which the lilac's numerous plume
Shook down perfume ;
Trim plots close blown
With daisies, in conspicuous myriads seen,
Engross'd each one
With single ardour for her spouse, the sun ;
Garths in their glad array
Of white and ruddy branch, auroral, gay,
With azure chill the maiden flow'r between ;
Meadows of fervid green,
With sometime sudden prospect of untold
Cowslips, like chance-found gold ;
And broadcast buttercups at joyful gaze,
Rending the air with praise,

AMELIA

Like the six-hundred-thousand-voiced shout
Of Jacob camp'd in Midian put to rout ;
Then through the Park,
Where Spring to livelier gloom
Quicken'd the cedars dark,
And, 'gainst the clear sky cold,
Which shone afar
Crowded with sunny alps oracular,
Great chestnuts raised themselves abroad like
    cliffs of bloom ;
And everywhere,
Amid the ceaseless rapture of the lark,
With wonder new
We caught the solemn voice of single air,
'Cuckoo !'

   .   .   .   .   .

Now would I keep my promise to her Mother ;
Now I arose, and raised her to her feet,
My best Amelia, fresh-born from a kiss,
Moth-like, full-blown in birthdew shuddering
    sweet,
With great, kind eyes, in whose brown shade
Bright Venus and her Baby play'd !
  At inmost heart well pleased with one
    another,
What time the slant sun low

Through the plough'd field does each clod sharply
    shew,
And softly fills
With shade the dimples of our homeward hills,
With little said,
We left the 'wilder'd garden of the dead,
And gain'd the gorse-lit shoulder of the down
That keeps the north-wind from the nestling
    town,
And caught, once more, the vision of the wave,
Where, on the horizon's dip,
A many-sailed ship
Pursued alone her distant purpose grave ;
And, by steep steps rock-hewn, to the dim street
I led her sacred feet ;
And so the Daughter gave,
Soft, moth-like, sweet,
Showy as damask-rose and shy as musk,
Back to her Mother, anxious in the dusk.
And now ' Good-night ! '
Me shall the phantom months no more affright.
For heaven's gates to open well waits he
Who keeps himself the key.

AFTER STORM

So lay the Earth that saw the skies
   Grow clear and bright above,
As the repentant spirit lies
   In God's forgiving love.
The lark forsook the waning day,
   And all loud songs did cease ;
The robin, from a wither'd spray,
   Sang like a soul at peace.
Far to the South, in sunset glow'd
   The peaks of Dartmoor ridge,
And Tamar, full and tranquil, flow'd
   Beneath the Gresson Bridge.
There, conscious of the numerous noise
   Of rain-awaken'd rills,
And gathering deep and sober joys
   From the heart-enlarging hills,
I sat, until the first white star
   Appear'd, with dewy rays,
And the fair moon began to bar

With shadows all the ways.
O, well is thee, whate'er thou art,
   And happy shalt thou be,
If thou hast known, within thy heart,
   The peace that came to me.
O, well is thee, if aught shall win
   Thy spirit to confess,
God proffers all, 'twere grievous sin
   To live content in less !

VENUS AND DEATH

WITH fetters gold her captivated feet
Lay, sunny sweet;
In that palm was the poppy, Sleep; in this
The apple, Bliss;
Against the mild side of his Spouse and Mother
One small God throve, and in't, meseem'd, another.
By these a Death-in-Life did foully breathe
Out of a face that was one grate of teeth.
Lift, O kind Angels, lift her eyelids loth,
Lest he devour her and her Godlets both !

SEMELE

No praise to me!
My joy 'twas to be nothing but the glass
Thro' which the general boon of Heaven should
    pass,
To focus upon thee.
Nor is't thy blame
Thou first should'st glow, and, after, fade i' the
    flame.
It takes more might
Than God has given thee, Dear, so long to feel
    delight.
Shall I, alas,
Reproach thee with thy change and my regret?
Blind fumblers that we be
About the portals of felicity!
The wind of words would scatter, tears would wash
Quite out the little heat
Beneath the silent and chill-seeming ash,
Perchance, still slumbering sweet.

THE MARRIED LOVER

Why, having won her, do I woo?
  Because her spirit's vestal grace
Provokes me always to pursue,
  But, spirit-like, eludes embrace ;
Because her womanhood is such
  That, as on court-days subjects kiss
The Queen's hand, yet so near a touch
  Affirms no mean familiarness,
Nay, rather marks more fair the height
  Which can with safety so neglect
To dread, as lower ladies might,
  That grace could meet with disrespect,
Thus she with happy favour feeds
  Allegiance from a love so high
That thence no false conceit proceeds
  Of difference bridged, or state put by ;
Because, although in act and word
  As lowly as a wife can be,
Her manners, when they call me lord,

THE MARRIED LOVER

Remind me 'tis by courtesy ;
Not with her least consent of will,
   Which would my proud affection hurt,
But by the noble style that still
   Imputes an unattain'd desert ;
Because her gay and lofty brows,
   When all is won which hope can ask,
Reflect a light of hopeless snows
   That bright in virgin ether bask ;
Because, though free of the outer court
   I am, this Temple keeps its shrine
Sacred to Heaven ; because, in short,
   She's not and never can be mine.

THE AMARANTH

Feasts satiate ; stars distress with height ;
    Friendship means well, but misses reach,
And wearies in its best delight
    Vex'd with the vanities of speech ;
Too long regarded, roses even
    Afflict the mind with fond unrest ;
And to converse direct with Heaven
    Is oft a labour in the breast ;
Whate'er the up-looking soul admires,
    Whate'er the senses' banquet be,
Fatigues at last with vain desires,
    Or sickens by satiety ;
But truly my delight was more
    In her to whom I'm bound for aye
Yesterday than the day before,
    And more to-day than yesterday.

THE LETTERS

Let me, Beloved, while gratitude
Is garrulous with coming good,
Or ere the tongue of happiness
Be silenced by your soft caress,
Relate how, musing here of you,
The clouds, the intermediate blue,
The air that rings with larks, the grave
And distant rumour of the wave,
The solitary sailing skiff,
The gusty corn-field on the cliff,
The corn-flower by the crumbling ledge,
Or, far-down at the shingle's edge,
The sighing sea's recurrent crest
Breaking, resign'd to its unrest,
All whisper, to my home-sick thought,
Of charms in you till now uncaught,
Or only caught as dreams, to die
Ere they were own'd by memory.
    High and ingenious Decree

Of joy-devising Deity !
You whose ambition only is
The assurance that you make my bliss,
(Hence my first debt of love to show
That you, past showing, indeed do so !)
Trust me, the world, the firmament,
With diverse-natured worlds besprent,
Were rear'd in no mere undivine
Boast of omnipotent design,
The lion differing from the snake
But for the trick of difference sake,
And comets darting to and fro
Because in circles planets go ;
But rather that sole love might be
Refresh'd throughout eternity
In one sweet faith, for ever strange,
Mirror'd by circumstantial change.
For, more and more, do I perceive
That everything is relative
To you, and that there's not a star,
Nor nothing in't, so strange or far,
But, if 'twere scanned, 'twould chiefly mean
Somewhat, till then, in you unseen,
Something to make the bondage strait
Of you and me more intimate,
Some unguess'd opportunity

Of nuptials in a new degree.

But, oh, with what a novel force
Your best-conn'd beauties, by remorse
Of absence, touch ; and, in my heart,
How bleeds afresh the youthful smart
Of passion fond, despairing still
To utter infinite good-will
By worthy service ! Yet I know
That love is all that love can owe,
And this to offer is no less
Of worth, in kind speech or caress,
Than if my life-blood I should give.
For good is God's prerogative,
And Love's deed is but to prepare
The flatter'd, dear Belov'd to dare
Acceptance of His gifts. When first
On me your happy beauty burst,
Honoria, verily it seem'd
That naught beyond you could be dream'd
Of beauty and of heaven's delight.
Zeal of an unknown infinite
Yet bade me ever wish you more
Beatified than e'er before.
Angelical were your replies
To my prophetic flatteries ;
And sweet was the compulsion strong

That drew me in the course along
Of heaven's increasing bright allure,
With provocations fresh of your
Victorious capacity.
Whither may love, so fledged, not fly?
    Did not mere Earth hold fast the string
Of this celestial soaring thing,
So measure and make sensitive,
And still, to the nerves, nice notice give
Of each minutest increment
Of such interminable ascent,
The heart would lose all count, and beat
Unconscious of a height so sweet,
And the spirit-pursuing senses strain
Their steps on the starry track in vain!
But, reading now the note just come,
With news of you, the babes, and home,
I think, and say, ' To-morrow eve
' With kisses me will she receive ; '
And, thinking, for extreme delight
Of love's extremes, I laugh outright.

    Dearest, my Love and Wife, 'tis long
Ago I closed the unfinish'd song
Which never could be finish'd ; nor
Will ever Poet utter more

Of love than I did, watching well
To lure to speech the unspeakable !
‘ *Why, having won her, do I woo ?* ’
That final strain to the last height flew
Of written joy, which wants the smile
And voice that are, indeed, the while
They last, the very things you speak,
Honoria, who mak'st music weak
With ways that say, ‘ Shall I not be
‘ As kind to all as Heaven to me ? ’
And yet, ah, twenty-fold my Bride !
Rising, this twentieth festal-tide,
You still soft sleeping, on this day
Of days, some words I long to say,
Some words superfluously sweet
Of fresh assurance, thus to greet
Your waking eyes, which never grow
Weary of telling what I know
So well, yet only well enough
To wish for further news thereof.

How sing of such things save to her,
Love's self, so love's interpreter ?
How the supreme rewards confess
Which crown the austere voluptuousness
Of heart, that earns, in midst of wealth,

The appetite of want and health,
Relinquishes the pomp of life
And beauty to the pleasant Wife
At home, and does all joy despise
As out of place but in her eyes?
How praise the years and gravity
That make each favour seem to be
A lovelier weakness for her lord?
And, ah, how find the tender word
To tell aright of love that glows
The fairer for the fading rose?
Of frailty which can weight the arm
To lean with thrice its girlish charm?
Of grace which, like this autumn day,
Is not the sad one of decay,
Yet one whose pale brow pondereth
The far-off majesty of death?
How tell the crowd, whom passion
    rends,
That love grows mild as it ascends?
That joy's most high and distant mood
Is lost, not found, in dancing blood;
Albeit kind acts and smiling eyes,
And all those fond realities
Which are love's words, in us mean more
Delight than twenty years before?

ONE SPRING

For many a dreadful day,
In sea-side lodgings sick she lay,
Noteless of love, nor seem'd to hear
The sea, on one side, thundering near,
Nor, on the other, the loud Ball
Held nightly in the public hall;
Nor vex'd they my short slumbers, though
I woke up if she breathed too low.
Thus, for three months, with terrors rife,
The pending of her precious life
I watch'd o'er; and the danger, at last,
The kind Physician said, was past.
Howbeit, for seven harsh weeks the East
Breathed witheringly, and Spring's growth
      ceased,
And so she only did not die;
Until the bright and blighting sky
Changed into cloud, and the sick flowers
Remember'd their perfumes, and showers

ONE SPRING

Of warm, small rain refreshing flew
Before the South, and the Park grew,
In three nights, thick with green.   Then she
Revived, no less than flower and tree,
In the mild air, and, the fourth day,
Look'd supernaturally gay
With large, thanksgiving eyes, that shone,
The while I tied her bonnet on,
So that I led her to the glass,
And bade her see how fair she was,
And how love visibly could shine.
Profuse of hers, desiring mine,
And mindful I had loved her most
When beauty seem'd a vanish'd boast,
She laugh'd.   I press'd her then to me,
Nothing but soft humility ;
Nor e'er enhanced she with such charms
Her acquiescence in my arms.

MA BELLE

FAREWELL, dear Heart! Since needs it must I
    go,
Dear Heart, farewell!
Fain would I stay, but that I love thee so.
One kiss, ma Belle!
What hope lies in the Land we do not know
Who, Dear, can tell?
But thee I love, and let thy plaint be, ' Lo,
He loved me well! '

A FAREWELL

With all my will, but much against my heart,
We two now part.
My Very Dear,
Our solace is, the sad road lies so clear.
It needs no art,
With faint, averted feet
And many a tear,
In our opposed paths to persevere.
Go thou to East, I West.
We will not say
There's any hope, it is so far away.
But, O, My Best,
When the one darling of our widowhead,
The nursling Grief,
Is dead,
And no dews blur our eyes
To see the peach-bloom come in evening skies,
Perchance we may,
Where now this night is day,

And even through faith of still averted feet,
Making full circle of our banishment,
Amazed meet ;
The bitter journey to the bourne so sweet
Seasoning the termless feast of our content
With tears of recognition never dry.

DEPARTURE

It was not like your great and gracious ways!
Do you, that have nought other to lament,
Never, my Love, repent
Of how, that July afternoon,
You went,
With sudden, unintelligible phrase,
And frighten'd eye,
Upon your journey of so many days,
Without a single kiss, or a good-bye?
I knew, indeed, that you were parting soon;
And so we sate, within the low sun's rays,
You whispering to me, for your voice was weak,
Your harrowing praise.
Well, it was well,
To hear you such things speak,
And I could tell
What made your eyes a growing gloom of love,
As a warm South-wind sombres a March grove.
And it was like your great and gracious ways

To turn your talk on daily things, my Dear,
Lifting the luminous, pathetic lash
To let the laughter flash,
Whilst I drew near,
Because you spoke so low that I could scarcely
    hear.
But all at once to leave me at the last,
More at the wonder than the loss aghast,
With huddled, unintelligible phrase,
And frighten'd eye,
And go your journey of all days
With not one kiss, or a good-bye,
And the only loveless look the look with which
    you pass'd :
"Twas all unlike your great and gracious ways.

THE AZALEA

There, where the sun shines first
Against our room,
She train'd the gold Azalea, whose perfume
She, Spring-like, from her breathing grace dis-
    persed.
Last night the delicate crests of saffron bloom,
For this their dainty likeness watch'd and nurst,
Were just at point to burst.
At dawn I dream'd, O God, that she was dead,
And groan'd aloud upon my wretched bed,
And waked, ah, God, and did not waken her,
But lay, with eyes still closed,
Perfectly bless'd in the delicious sphere
By which I knew so well that she was near,
My heart to speechless thankfulness composed.
Till 'gan to stir
A dizzy somewhat in my troubled head—
It *was* the azalea's breath, and she *was* dead!
The warm night had the lingering buds disclosed,

And I had fall'n asleep with to my breast
A chance-found letter press'd
In which she said,
'So, till to-morrow eve, my Own, adieu!
Parting's well-paid with soon again to meet,
Soon in your arms to feel so small and sweet,
Sweet to myself that am so sweet to you!'

EURYDICE

Is this the portent of the day nigh past,
And of a restless grave
O'er which the eternal sadness gathers fast;
Or but the heaped wave
Of some chance, wandering tide,
Such as that world of awe
Whose circuit, listening to a foreign law,
Conjunctures ours at unguess'd dates and wide,
Does in the Spirit's tremulous ocean draw,
To pass unfateful on, and so subside?
Thee, whom ev'n more than Heaven loved I
  have,
And yet have not been true
Even to thee,
I, dreaming, night by night, seek now to see,
And, in a mortal sorrow, still pursue
Thro' sordid streets and lanes
And houses brown and bare
And many a haggard stair

Ochrous with ancient stains,
And infamous doors, opening on hapless rooms,
In whose unhaunted glooms
Dead pauper generations, witless of the sun,
Their course have run ;
And ofttimes my pursuit
Is check'd of its dear fruit
By things brimful of hate, my kith and kin,
Furious that I should keep
Their forfeit power to weep,
And mock, with living fear, their mournful malice
 thin.
But ever, at the last, my way I win
To where, with perfectly sad patience, nurst
By sorry comfort of assured worst,
Ingrain'd in fretted cheek and lips that pine,
On pallet poor
Thou lyest, stricken sick,
Beyond love's cure,
By all the world's neglect, but chiefly mine.
Then sweetness, sweeter than my tongue can
 tell,
Does in my bosom well,
And tears come free and quick
And more and more abound
For piteous passion keen at having found,

EURYDICE

After exceeding ill, a little good ;
A little good
Which, for the while,
Fleets with the current sorrow of the blood,
Though no good here has heart enough to smile.

THE DAY AFTER
TO-MORROW

PERCHANCE she droops within the hollow gulf
Which the great wave of coming pleasure draws,
Not guessing the glad cause !
Ye Clouds that on your endless journey go,
Ye Winds that westward flow,
Thou heaving Sea
That heav'st 'twixt her and me,
Tell her I come ;
Then only sigh your pleasure, and be dumb ;
For the sweet secret of our either self
We know.
Tell her I come,
And let her heart be still'd.
One day's controlled hope, and then one more,
And on the third our lives shall be fulfill'd !
Yet all has been before :
Palm placed in palm, twin smiles, and words
        astray.
What other should we say ?

THE DAY AFTER TO-MORROW

But shall I not, with ne'er a sign, perceive,
Whilst her sweet hands I hold,
The myriad threads and meshes manifold
Which Love shall round her weave:
The pulse in that vein making alien pause
And varying beats from this;
Down each long finger felt, a diff'ring strand
Of silvery welcome bland;
And in her breezy palm
And silken wrist,
Beneath the touch of my like numerous bliss
Complexly kiss'd,
A diverse and distinguishable calm?
What should we say!
It all has been before;
And yet our lives shall now be first fulfill'd,
And into their summ'd sweetness fall distill'd
One sweet drop more;
One sweet drop more, in absolute increase
Of unrelapsing peace.
    O, heaving Sea,
That heav'st as if for bliss of her and me,
And separatest not dear heart from heart,
Though each 'gainst other beats too far apart,
For yet awhile
Let it not seem that I behold her smile.

O, weary Love, O, folded to her breast,
Love in each moment years and years of rest,
Be calm, as being not.
Ye oceans of intolerable delight,
The blazing photosphere of central Night,
Be ye forgot.
Terror, thou swarthy Groom of Bride-bliss coy,
Let me not see thee toy.
O, Death, too tardy with thy hope intense
Of kisses close beyond conceit of sense ;
O, Life, too liberal, while to take her hand
Is more of hope than heart can understand ;
Perturb my golden patience not with joy,
Nor, through a wish, profane
The peace that should pertain
To him who does by her attraction move.
Has all not been before ?
One day's controlled hope, and one again,
And then the third, and ye shall have the rein,
O Life, Death, Terror, Love !
But soon let your unrestful rapture cease,
Ye flaming Ethers thin,
Condensing till the abiding sweetness win
One sweet drop more ;
One sweet drop more in the measureless increase
Of honied peace.

TIRED MEMORY

THE stony rock of death's insensibility
Well'd yet awhile with honey of thy love
And then was dry;
Nor could thy picture, nor thine empty glove,
Nor all thy kind, long letters, nor the band
Which really spann'd
Thy body chaste and warm,
Henceforward move
Upon the stony rock their wearied charm.
At last, then, thou wast dead.
Yet would I not despair,
But wrought my daily task, and daily said
Many and many a fond, unfeeling prayer,
To keep my vows of faith to thee from harm
In vain.
' For 'tis,' I said, ' all one,
The wilful faith, which has no joy or pain,
As if 'twere none.'
Then look'd I miserably round

If aught of duteous love were left undone,
And nothing found.
But, kneeling in a Church one Easter-Day,
It came to me to say :
' Though there is no intelligible rest,
In Earth or Heaven,
For me, but on her breast,
I yield her up, again to have her given,
Or not, as, Lord, Thou wilt, and that for aye.'
And the same night, in slumber lying,
I, who had dream'd of thee as sad and sick and
        dying,
And only so, nightly for all one year,
Did thee, my own most Dear,
Possess,
In gay, celestial beauty nothing coy,
And felt thy soft caress
With heretofore unknown reality of joy.
But, in our mortal air,
None thrives for long upon the happiest dream,
And fresh despair
Bade me seek round afresh for some extreme
Of unconceiv'd, interior sacrifice
Whereof the smoke might rise
To God, and 'mind him that one pray'd below.
And so,

TIRED MEMORY

In agony, I cried :
' My Lord, if thy strange will be this,
That I should crucify my heart,
Because my love has also been my pride,
I do submit, if I saw how, to bliss
Wherein She has no part.'
And I was heard,
And taken at my own remorseless word.
O, my most Dear,
Was't treason, as I fear ?
'Twere that, and worse, to plead thy veiled mind,
Kissing thy babes, and murmuring in mine ear,
' Thou canst not be
Faithful to God, and faithless unto me !'
Ah, prophet kind !
I heard, all dumb and blind
With tears of protest ; and I cannot see
But faith was broken.   Yet, as I have said,
My heart was dead,
Dead of devotion and tired memory,
When a strange grace of thee
In a fair stranger, as I take it, bred
To her some tender heed,
Most innocent
Of purpose therewith blent,
And pure of faith, I think, to thee ; yet such

That the pale reflex of an alien love,
So vaguely, sadly shown,
Did her heart touch
Above
All that, till then, had wooed her for its own.
And so the fear, which is love's chilly dawn,
Flush'd faintly upon lids that droop'd like thine,
And made me weak,
By thy delusive likeness doubly drawn,
And Nature's long suspended breath of flame
Persuading soft, and whispering Duty's name,
Awhile to smile and speak
With this thy Sister sweet, and therefore mine ;
Thy Sister sweet,
Who bade the wheels to stir
Of sensitive delight in the poor brain,
Dead of devotion and tired memory,
So that I lived again,
And, strange to aver,
With no relapse into the void inane,
For thee ;
But (treason was't ?) for thee and also her.

THE TOYS

My little Son, who look'd from thoughtful eyes
And moved and spoke in quiet grown-up wise,
Having my law the seventh time disobey'd,
I struck him, and dismiss'd
With hard words and unkiss'd,
His Mother, who was patient, being dead.
Then, fearing lest his grief should hinder sleep,
I visited his bed,
But found him slumbering deep,
With darken'd eyelids, and their lashes yet
From his late sobbing wet.
And I, with moan,
Kissing away his tears, left others of my own ;
For, on a table drawn beside his head,
He had put, within his reach,
A box of counters, and a red-vein'd stone,
A piece of glass abraded by the beach
And six or seven shells,
A bottle with bluebells

And two French copper coins, rang'd there with
    careful art,
To comfort his sad heart.
So when that night I pray'd
To God, I wept, and said:
Ah, when at last we lie with tranced breath,
Not vexing Thee in death,
And Thou rememberest of what toys
We made our joys,
How weakly understood,
Thy great commanded good,
Then, fatherly not less
Than I whom Thou hast moulded from the clay,
Thou'lt leave Thy wrath, and say,
' I will be sorry for their childishness.'

WINTER

I, SINGULARLY moved
To love the lovely that are not beloved,
Of all the Seasons, most
Love Winter, and to trace
The sense of the Trophonian pallor on her face.
It is not death, but plenitude of peace ;
And the dim cloud that does the world enfold
Hath less the characters of dark and cold
Than warmth and light asleep,
And correspondent breathing seems to keep
With the infant harvest, breathing soft below
Its eider coverlet of snow.
Nor is in field or garden anything
But, duly look'd into, contains serene
The substance of things hoped for, in the Spring,
And evidence of Summer not yet seen.
On every chance-mild day
That visits the moist shaw,
The honeysuckle, 'sdaining to be crost

In urgence of sweet life by sleet or frost,
'Voids the time's law
With still increase
Of leaflet new, and little, wandering spray;
Often, in sheltering brakes,
As one from rest disturb'd in the first hour,
Primrose or violet bewilder'd wakes,
And deems 'tis time to flower;
Though not a whisper of her voice he hear,
The buried bulb does know
The signals of the year,
And hails far Summer with his lifted spear.
The gorse-field dark, by sudden, gold caprice,
Turns, here and there, into a Jason's fleece;
Lilies, that soon in Autumn slipp'd their gowns of
    green,
And vanish'd into earth,
And came again, ere Autumn died, to birth,
Stand full-array'd, amidst the wavering shower,
And perfect for the Summer, less the flower;
In nook of pale or crevice of crude bark,
Thou canst not miss,
If close thou spy, to mark
The ghostly chrysalis,
That, if thou touch it, stirs in its dream dark:
And the flush'd Robin, in the evenings hoar,

WINTER

Does of Love's Day, as if he saw it, sing ;
But sweeter yet than dream or song of Summer
    or Spring
Are Winter's sometime smiles, that seem to well
From infancy ineffable ;
Her wandering, languorous gaze,
So unfamiliar, so without amaze,
On the elemental, chill adversity,
The uncomprehended rudeness ; and her sigh
And solemn, gathering tear,
And look of exile from some great repose, the
    sphere
Of ether, moved by ether only, or
By something still more tranquil.

L'ALLEGRO

FELICITY !
Who ope'st to none that knocks, yet, laughing weak,
Yield'st all to Love that will not seek,
And who, though won, wilt droop and die,
Unless wide doors bespeak thee free,
How safe's the bond of thee and me,
Since thee I cherish and defy !
Is't Love or Friendship, Dearest, we obey ?
Ah, thou art young, and I am gray ;
But happy man is he who knows
How well time goes,
With no unkind intruder by,
Between such friends as thou and I !
'Twould wrong thy favour, Sweet, were I to say,
'Tis best by far,
When best things are not possible,
To make the best of those that are ;
For, though it be not May,
Sure, few delights of Spring excel

L'ALLEGRO

The beauty of this mild September day !
So with me walk,
And view the dreaming field and bossy Autumn
    wood,
And how in humble russet goes
The Spouse of Honour, fair Repose,
Far from a world whence love is fled
And truth is dying because joy is dead;
And, if we hear the roaring wheel
Of God's remoter service, public zeal,
Let us to stiller place retire
And glad admire
How, near Him, sounds of working cease
In little fervour and much peace ;
And let us talk
Of holy things in happy mood,
Learnt of thy blest twin-sister, Certitude ;
Or let's about our neighbours chat,
Well praising this, less praising that,
And judging outer strangers by
Those gentle and unsanction'd lines
To which remorse of equity
Of old hath moved the School divines.
Or linger where this willow bends,
And let us, till the melody be caught,
Hearken that sudden, singing thought,

On which unguess'd increase to life perchance
    depends.
He ne'er hears twice the same who hears
The songs of heaven's unanimous spheres,
And this may be the song to make, at last, amends
For many sighs and boons in vain long sought !

A RETROSPECT

I, TRUSTING that the truly sweet
  Would still be sweetly found the true,
Sang, darkling, taught by heavenly heat,
  Songs which were wiser than I knew.
To the unintelligible dream
  That melted like a gliding star,
I said : 'We part to meet, fair Gleam !
  You are eternal, for you *are*.'
To Love's strange riddle, fiery writ
  In flesh and spirit of all create,
' Mocker,' I said, ' of mortal wit,
  Me you shall not mock.   I can wait.'

Printed by BALLANTYNE, HANSON & Co.
London & Edinburgh